Nadia Malik was born in South East
and Indonesian decent. Nadia write
she writes about identity, family, hon
Nadia is currently preparing to be
lives in London, where she raises
mother.

Venus Shells

Nadia Malik

Burning Eye

BurningEyeBooks
Never Knowingly
Mainstream

This edition published by Burning Eye Books 2018

www.burningeye.co.uk

@burningeyebooks

Burning Eye Books
15 West Hill, Portishead, BS20 6LG

ISBN 978-1-911570-55-4

Venus Shells

For those hurt and healing

CONTENTS

BUAH HATIKU

when my grandmother fell in the market
she refused to get up
she planted her head into the ground
and from it grew coconuts
from her hair
green grass grew
from her breasts
fruit plants
from her thighs
grew bamboo
and from her crotch kawung
I remember her in her sheer robe
warning my grandfather
you'll be sorry when I'm gone

LISTEN

if you stop ignoring the cry of your heart
you start to notice other sounds
passing cars like rolling waves
and the birds' eternal song
that carried on
through the years
you ignored it

LEARNING TO PRONOUNCE MY NAME

the first time I hear my name
through the wall of my mother's womb
it ripples

the first time I hear my name
from my father's scold
it falls

the first time I hear my name
through your voice in my ear
it sighs

the first time I hear my name
through my daughter's mouth
it cries

WATERMELON

do you know what it feels like
to squeeze yourself out
like toothpaste up from the toes
all your water flows
do you know what it feels like
to remove life from your body
energy that you carry
comes crying out of you
do you know what it feels like
to feel ripe and full and
know your own power

CRASH

this city's a sleepwalker
running
blind in the cold light
night forever
lit up
little roots poke through pavement cracks
the birds sing at midnight
street lights like artificial sunrise
people have bulbs for eyes
boys hide in matt black
they don't reflect
they project
anger
protect themselves from being accepted
into a system
that would break them
that would transform their hands
into claws to grip pens
to write in someone else's language
mothers ache for them
break bread and their backs for them
work the jobs they would never do
if they didn't have more than one soul to feed
and of course they bleed
willingly
and unwillingly
the way women do
but when their boys bleed too
they shatter
like a windshield

HOME

loneliness in the night city
is my kind of freedom
the cloak of the dark
turns street lights ethereal
the strangeness of strangers
is familiar to me
I feel no fear
as the canal fractures the moon
ripples it into dozens of silver slivers
wrinkles the tips of my fingers

SPRAY

we're not painted in the dappled postcard views
but stippled in the background of the six o'clock news
the south sun warms the cracked
paving stones and
heels and hands and
phones and
crippled hands loosen their grip
they have nothing to lose
no one watches
the losers
users
abusers
but when they shout and fight
and catch things with lighters
the flames writer paints his name in the sky
and I
with my little bruises choose to be alone and unseen
between frames and flames and hands with grappling brushes
grabbing at the frame
painting their name
in something permanent like blood
somewhere permanent like
the screens of the TVs whose
dappled movies everyone sees
and please just ignore me
hardly part of the story
you'll never see

PENDULUM

with your hand over my mouth
I sway like the pendulum moon
but I won't fall asleep
the smell of white spirit makes me dizzy
but I won't fall asleep
your white van sways as you cradle my throat
but I won't fall asleep
I don't tell anyone
I keep you with me long after you are gone
you come when I fall asleep

PINCH ITCH

I have milk skin
my grandma picks it like the paddy
between finger and thumb
she holds me
in the fields ingrained on her face
sweaty and comforting
like overcooked rice pudding

I AM YOUR GHOST

when you lie down at night
I am in the small space between your ribs
and the bedsprings
the memory you tell yourself is a dream
you breathe in deep
but there's a space the air can't reach
this is the space you wrote my name
always on the tip of your tongue
but you can't think of it
only your muscles remember
in the night
your hands grasp empty space
shaped like my throat
I am your ghost

MEDICINE

fear lives in my belly
and pain lives in my chest
I can't kill fear with food
but it helps me to digest it
like how oxygen doesn't numb pain
it just makes it easier to bear

I STOLE YOUR MUM'S SHOES
FROM MORNING PRAYER

your mother's yellow pedicure is chipped
like dried banana
she rises and falls
like a full moon
on a prayer mat
your mother's shoes are cracked
like old crows' feet
I put them on
like someone else's smell
I put my fists up my top and stretch it forward
like an expectant boxer
I imagine you are small enough to fit in my stomach
and I am your protector
I go home in shoes three sizes too big
feet like bananas
I imagine the day I am ripe

MAMA

my mother braids her hair
with one hand
cracks an apple
between her thighs
and rolls her eyes back
out of her head

STREET LIGHT GOING OUT

under the street corner light
in saying goodbye
in this moment
we are beginning and ending
we are a star that died a hundred years ago
and someone is wishing on us tonight
I am only this
I am two fingers
a kiss
your lips
and my cheek

THE MOON IN THE RIVER

tonight I am rounded
belly up to the sky
the river sighs slowly beside me
as it carries the moon
in its reflection
I am stillness
in action
I am building a home
without moving

MANMADE FIRE

in my home across the sea
the trees frequently blaze
like they're addicted
they suck themselves down
like cigarettes
ash drops on the ground
in the lungs
but no smoke gets in my eyes
I've won the prize of distance
we are far enough away
we can choose to be blind
I wonder
what's the word for invisible fire
but it still burns
and turns the trees to kindling

TIDES

all sisters
skyward together
gaze
at woman's waning curve
glowing us home
in the unforgetting darkness
that conjoins us
deep in the hip
darkness
drips
forever changing
round and waning
the same moon

WAITING

I'm weighted
in green eroded space
my feet tied to the sky
in seductive knots
I'm sedated

BEATS

I break my heart
like a 4/4 beat
I drop it
pick it up
drop it
repeat

BABY LAUGH

oh my little volcano
rumble up me
like unbearable laughter
burn me
like the moon's daughter
the first time she saw the sun

TRANSFORMATION

I am mummified
some kind of soft monster
pacified
muslin grows
under my toenails
baby pink
my bones are banished
I remove my chattering teeth
fill myself with rattle beans
soft shake and soothe
my soft toy limbs

YOU MAKE ME

how do you make me
small and big
simultaneously
I feel like the tiny hair
standing up on your neck
and
a static lion's mane
the storm excites
I feel like
a child who's never seen nothingness
and
a mother who can grow the world

DORMANT

remember
when I met you in the dark
your cigarette sparked
your haircut buzzed
you set me alight
and when the baby came
you left in the night
it's alright
you go back to being dormant
we have our own fire

LITTLE ONE

hold my hand
between the pavement cracks
whilst you're still small enough
to fall through

WANDER

I'm dancing syncopated tonight
in the in-between
the empty street
yellow lamps falling into blue light
the sound of my step
step
swallowed by silence
I think about the empty space
in my pockets
does it belong to me

COLOUR

I pour from a paint tube
in his gripping hand
yellow and pink
under pale knuckles
I am not blushing
under his gaze
he pours his pain into me
grey
he knows his paint can't capture me
but he tries anyway
from his fingers
I come out blue
confused
a mess like me but
simplified
he can't see the true colour of my eyes
he paints me in two dimensions
like he is removing my organs
so I learn to live without them
one day they will grow back
he can't take from me what he lacks

BODY

I am soft segments
between fragmenting fingers
leaning into me
a suspended meaning
lingering relentlessly

UNTOUCHABLE

this is the last day I am untouchable
this the day I learn about touch
not always soft
for twelve years my body belonged to me
the hills of my shoulder blades
and stomach planes
remained untrodden
today I feel a stranger walking up me
I cannot think
can only feel
wrinkled flesh meeting baby hair
wriggling fingers between my thighs
I leave without crying
without bruises
I go back to being a child
without realising
this was the last day I was untouchable

PARTS

I have no consistency
I'm like water but smoother
then I'm not
I've got a lot of body parts
and words
to throw around
I can lay myself out like a pack of cards
or wolves

SHAPE

I am tumult
shaped like woman
this is my power
today I will sit on the windowsill
in my white shirt
and that is the work
I will watch the warm morning light
so gently push through the shutters
I have no time for work that matters
the cool air lifting little hairs on my skin
is the revolution

TONGUE OF THE DRAGON

this boy
says he has a dragon tongue
he is too hard
to rest on
using kisses like a key
his persistent tongue
trying fragility
pops like gum

PORCELAIN

I drink tea
lip to bone china lip
the roses in my cheeks show
I face the sun
with unprotected skin
darkening as she burnishes me
I am her artwork
porcelain painted

DREAMS

new mothers don't sleep and wake
they die and come back to life
I couldn't learn to sleep
until I learnt to be tired
I don't dream anymore
but I exist in this subconscious world
of exhaustion and devotion
I have a new perspective
like night vision
the space that I write in
where my eyes don't hide from the truth
where I can be ugly
and love it too
nightmare monsters
become friends
and when it ends
it ends
and I sleep peacefully
like in death

GRAIN

a single mother
like a grain of rice
the world rested
in her hand

AWARE

I can't see underwater in the ocean
without getting salt in my eyes
the beauty stings
but I refuse to swim blind

INSOMNIA GAME

sleep crystallises in my eyes
I wear them
like sugared almonds
looks
I throw like money
and count
the bleating years
that slip through my fingers
like cheap sheets
I bite
and stain

THOUGHTS

a bird soars
on roaring waves
makes me think of you
for no other reason than
everything makes me think of you
eventually

LOVE

I gently let go of your hand
let you stand alone
I watch as the rain beats down on you
I'm here
when you come looking
for the shelter of my arms

ACKNOWLEDGEMENTS

To the Malik-Pearson family and Chantelle, Helen and Sean thank you for loving me through it all.